Stars and Spots

Written by Gill Munton
Illustrated by Amelia Rosato

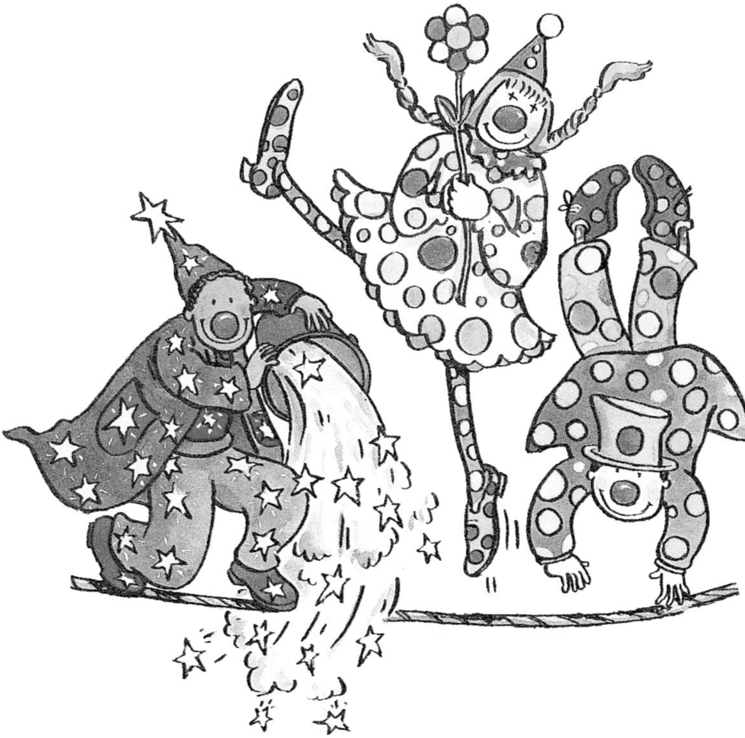

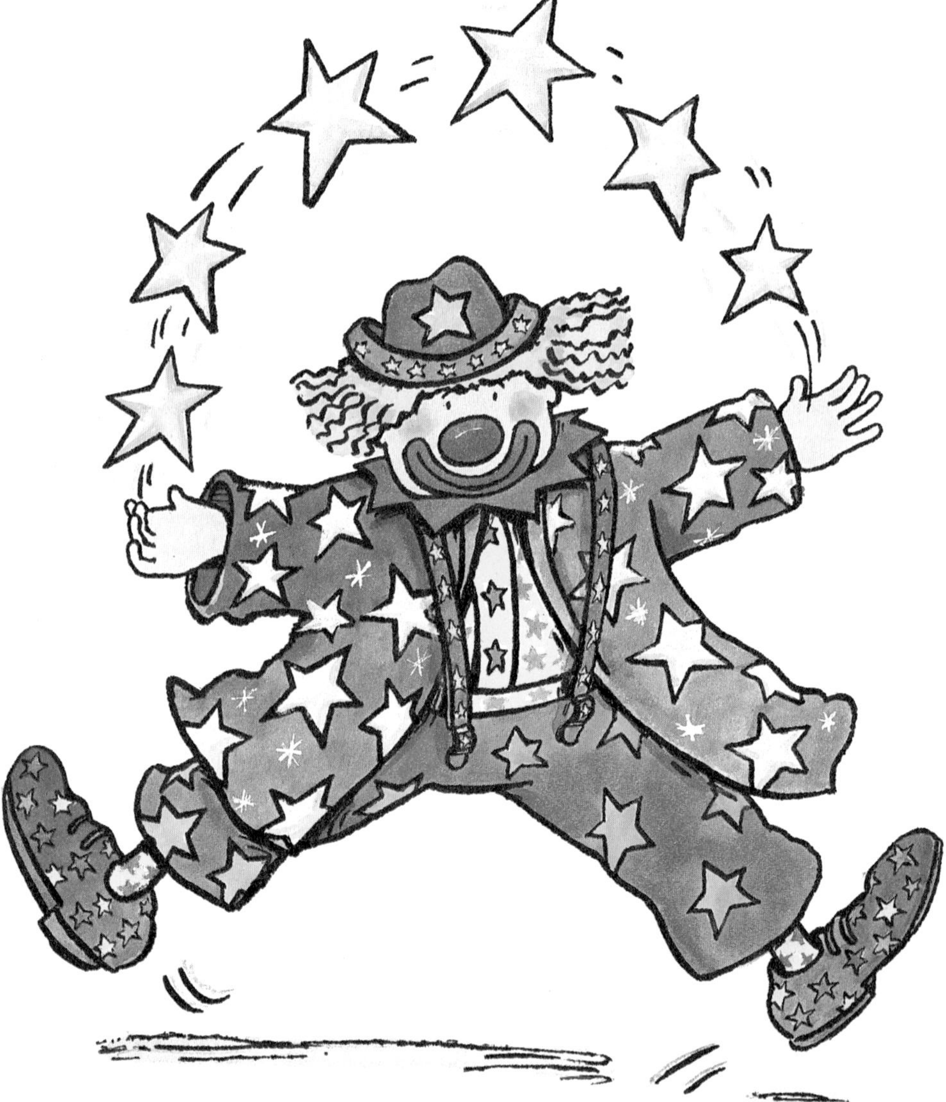

stars

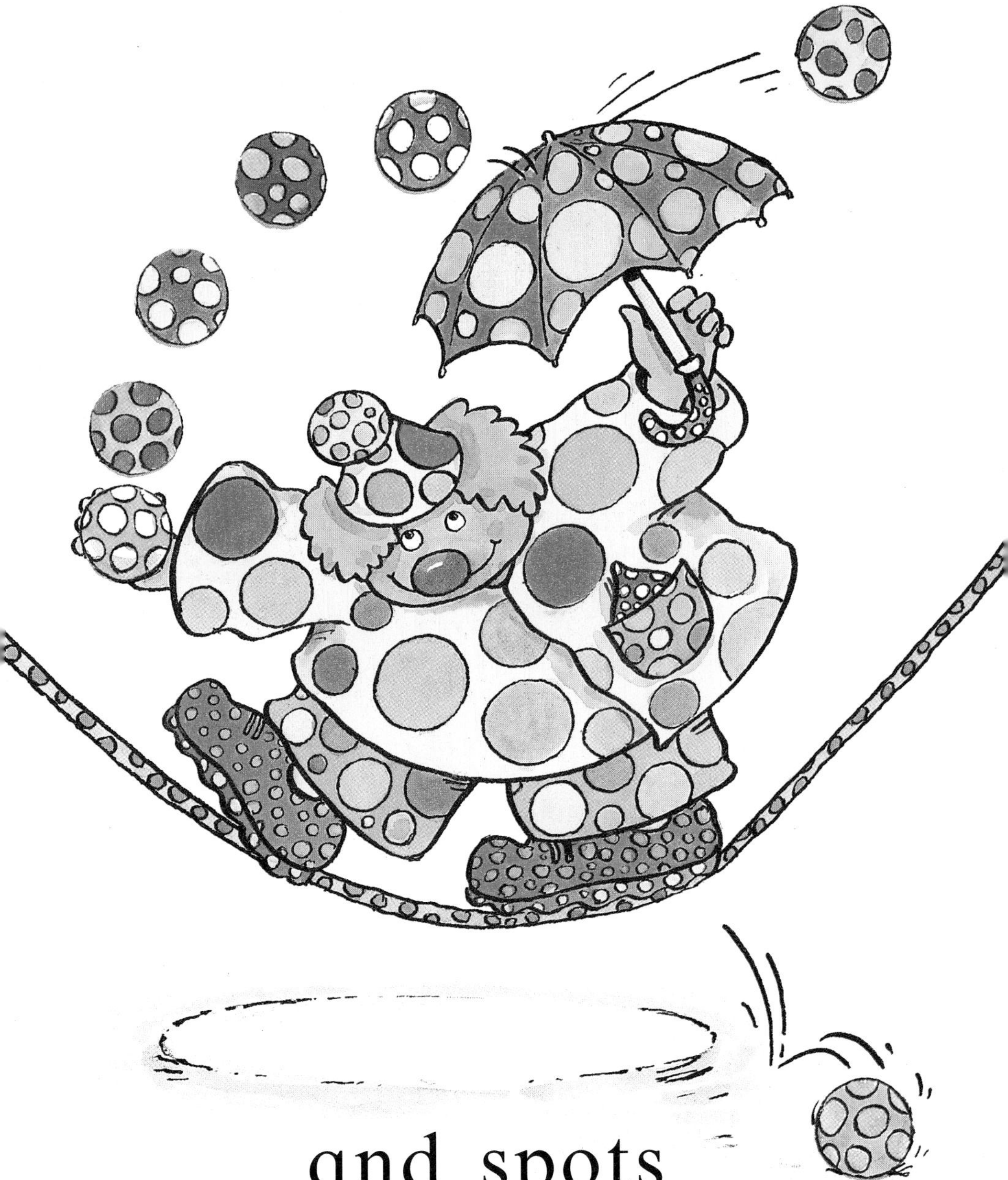

and spots

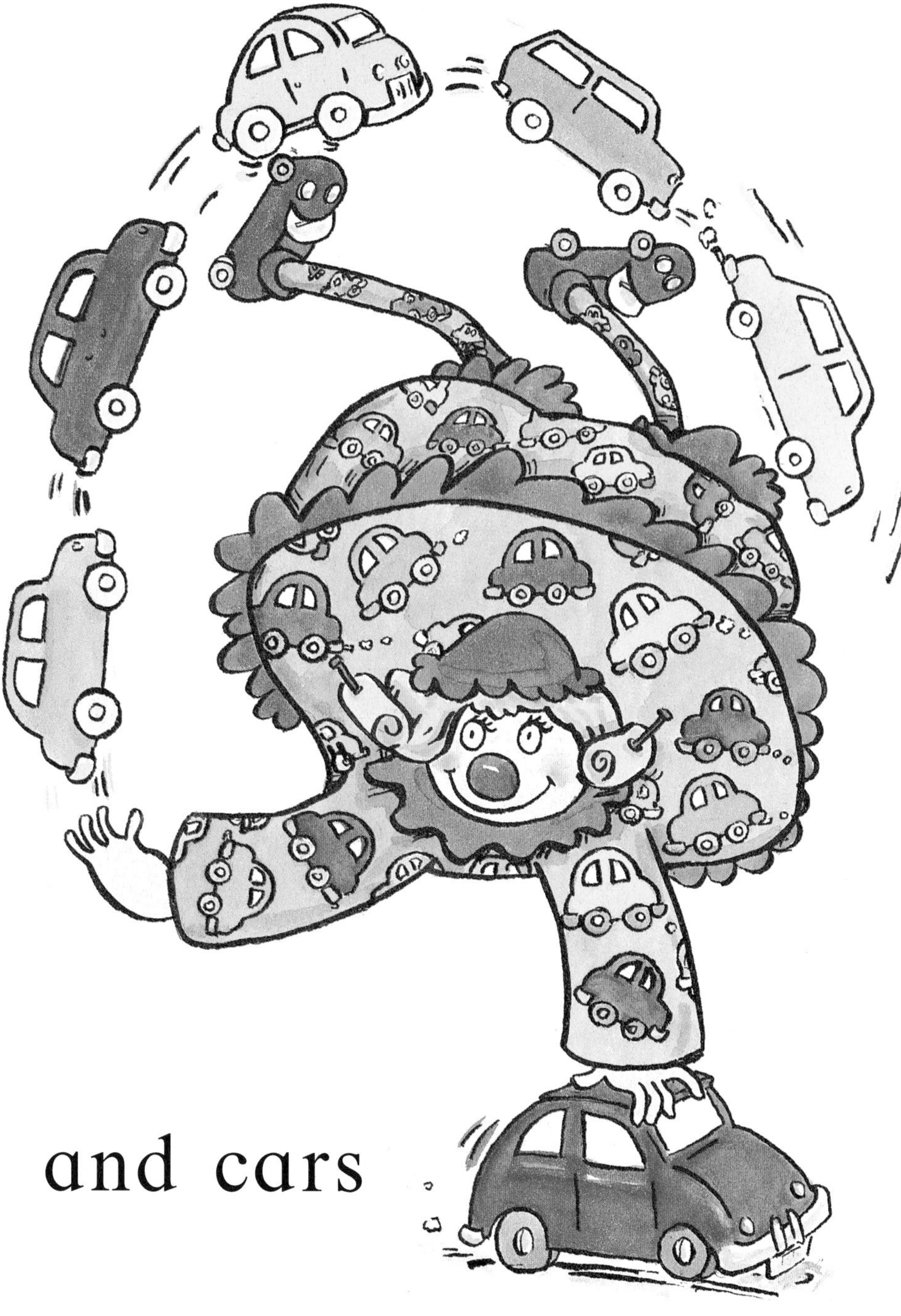

and cars

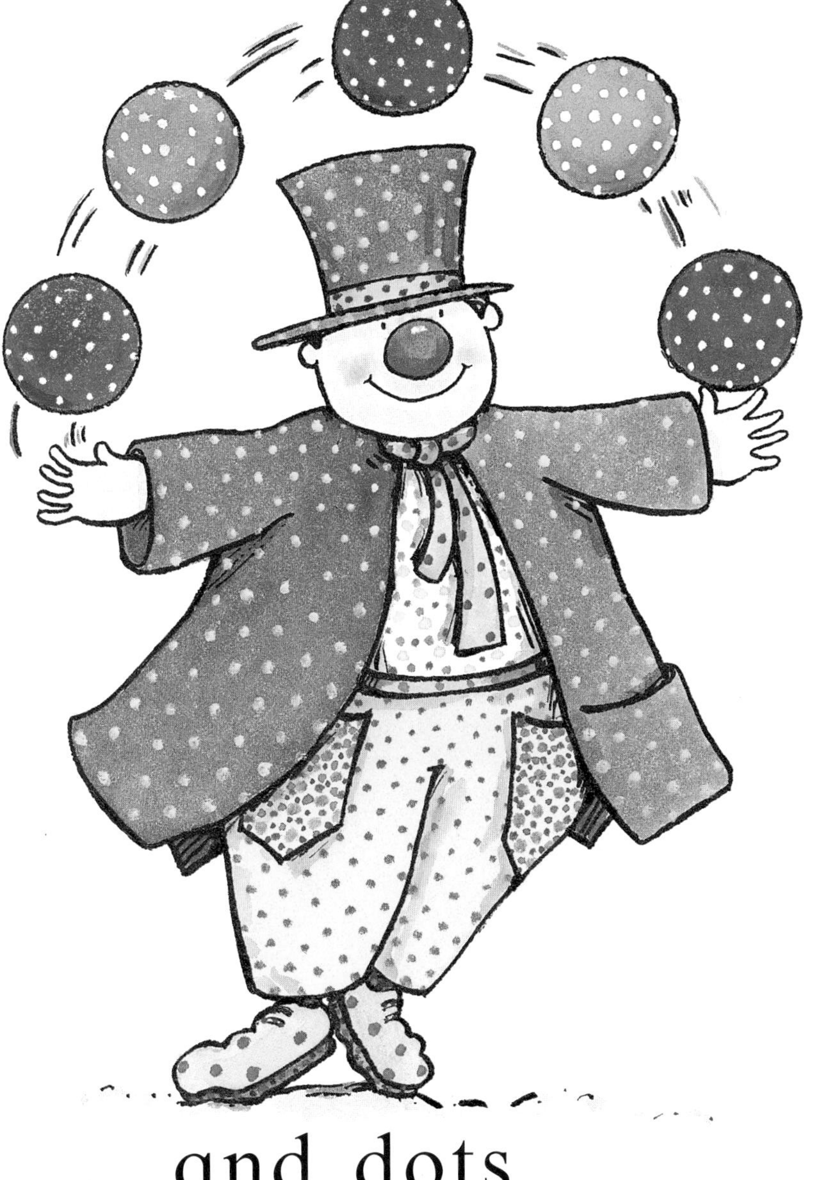

and dots

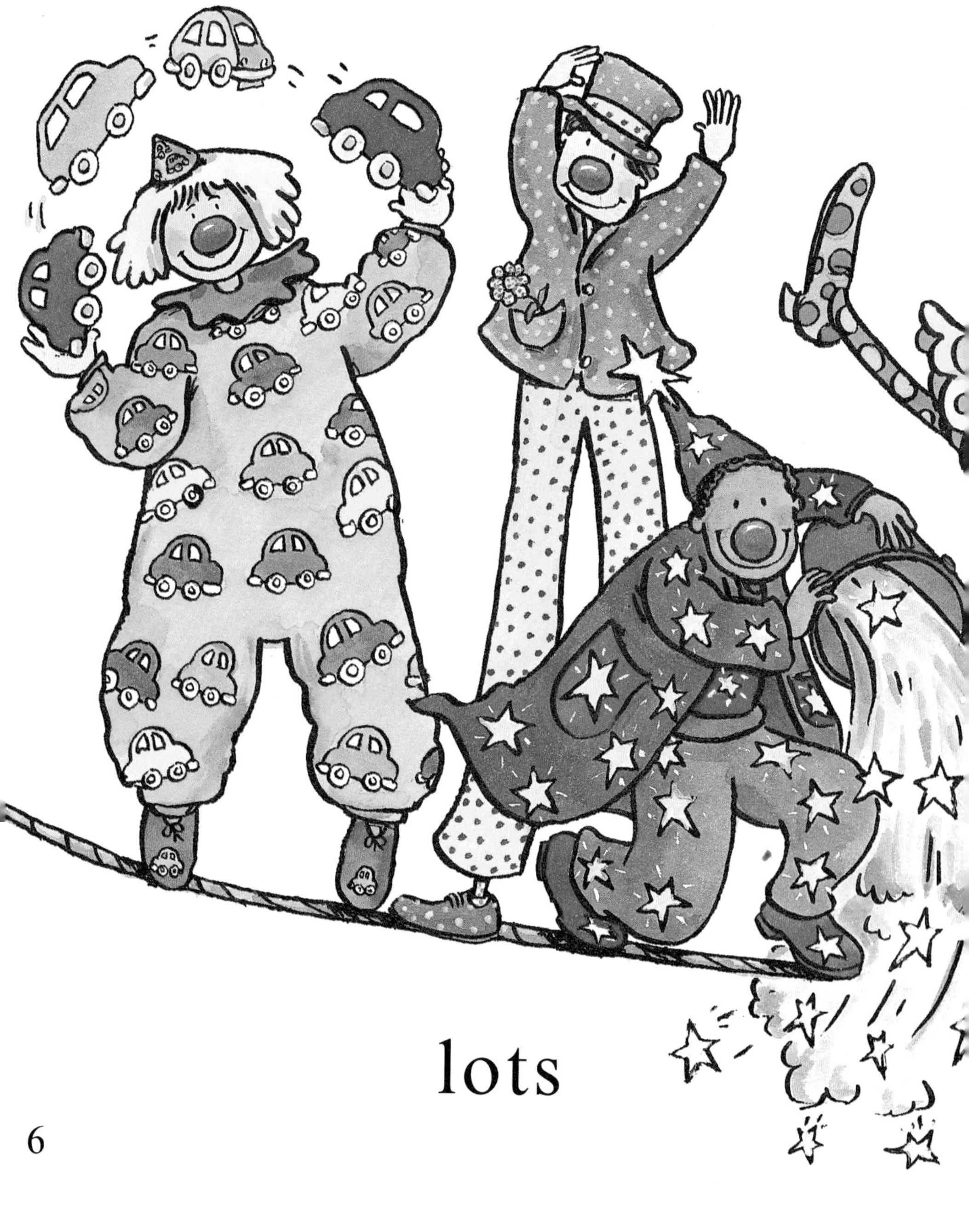

lots

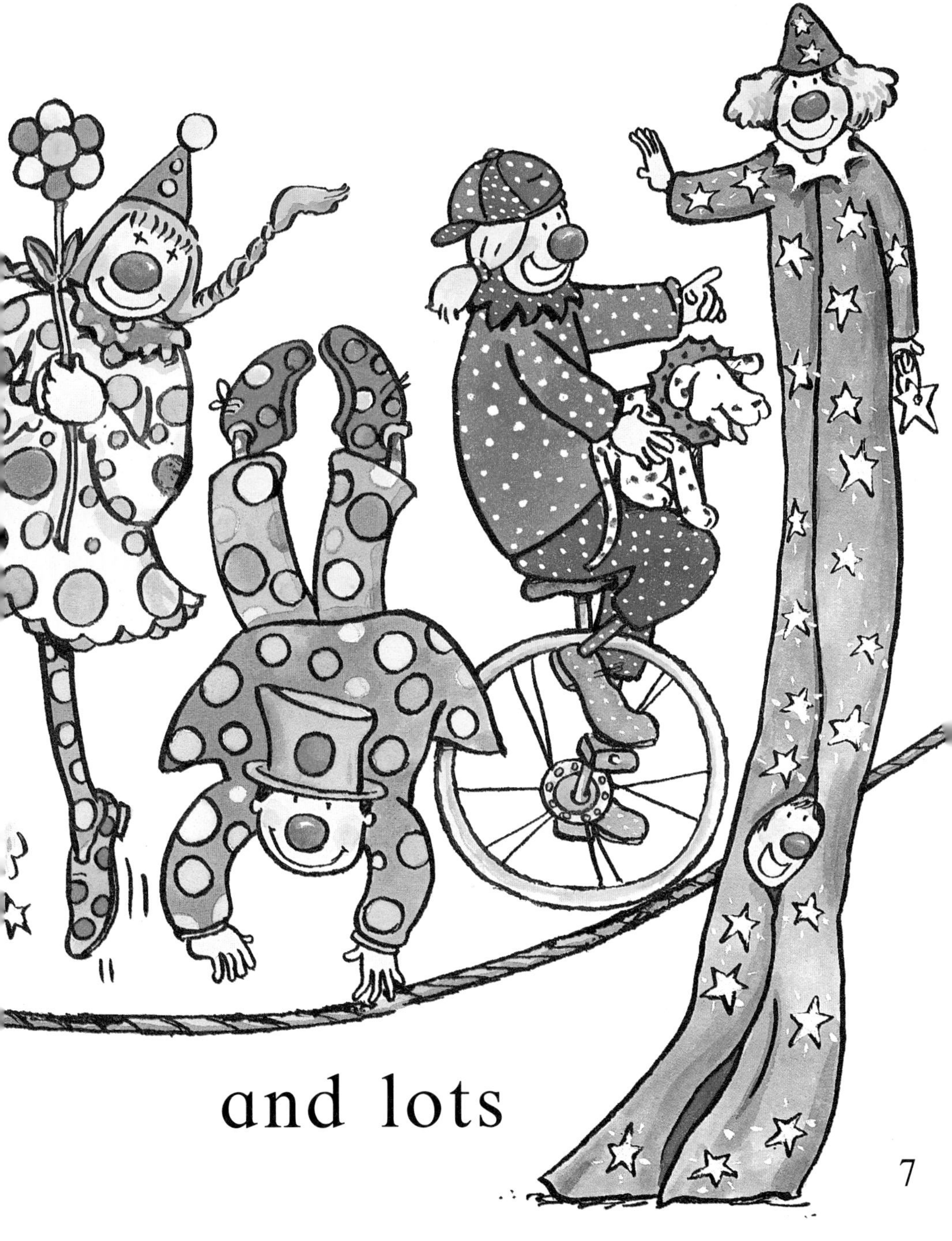

and lots

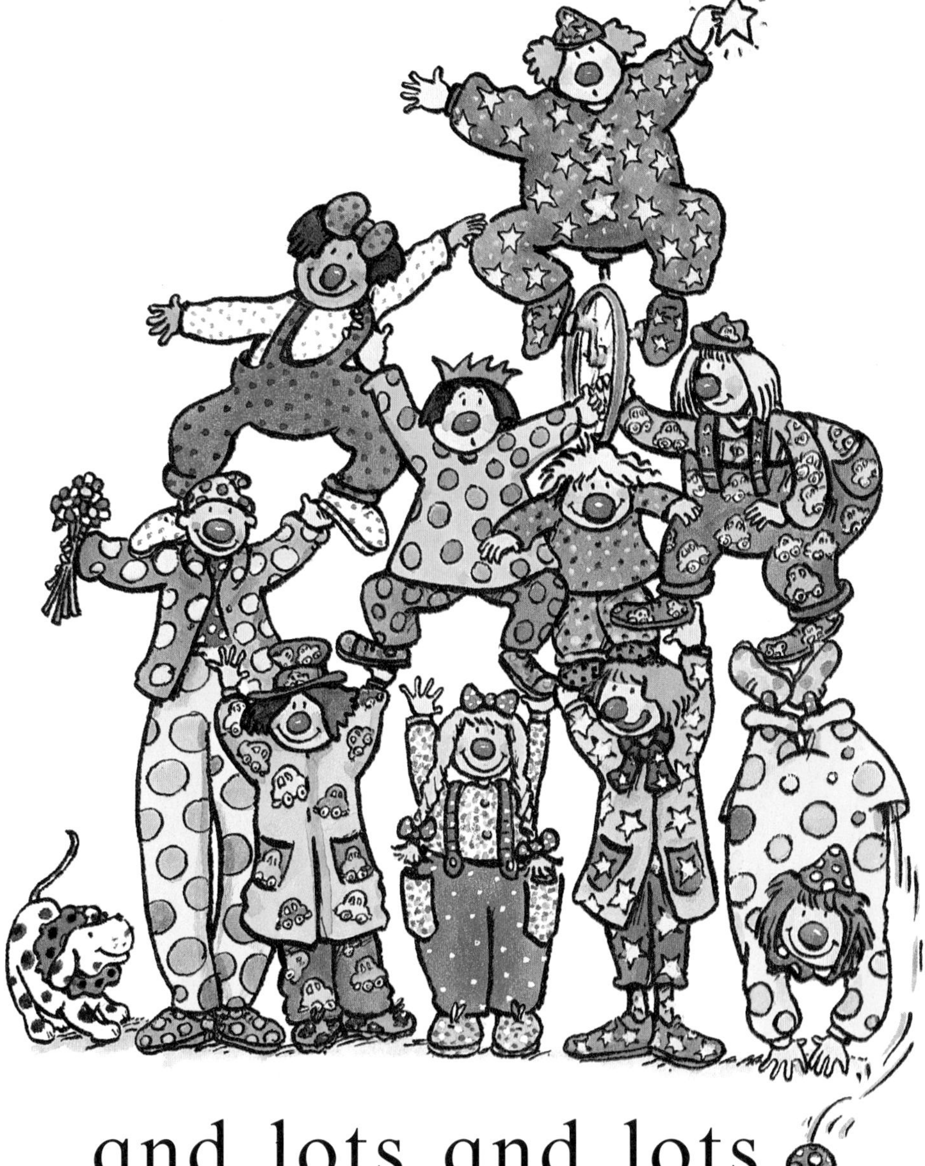

and lots and lots